Human Dignity Is Inviolable

Text - Collection

AUTHOR / PICTURES /
COVER

DIRK L. FEILER

1. MY OLD PRINTER

MY OLD PRINTER WROTE : THE SIMPLICITY REMAINS ... I TALK TO THE BEINGS THAT EXIST IN THE BODY THAT NEED TO DIE TO HELP US DO THIS BECAUSE WE BELIEVED . THIS " SCAVENGER CELLS " WERE VERY UPSET TO

HAVE TO DO THIS INCOMPREHENSIBLE WORK, DURING THE FIRST CONVERSATION WITH SUCH A CREATURE I CAME ON STRONG AGAIN WAS - UNTIL I STILL GOT OWNED - THE ENTITY EXPRESSED A KIND OF AMAZEMENT , HENCE WHY I THAT EVER ASKED BECAUSE THESE BEINGS AND THEREFORE HAVE NO IDEA WHY THEY NEED TO EXIST BECAUSE

THEIR WORK DID NOT MAKE SENSE - THE PLANET IS MADE OF A NON- DETECTABLE REASON PRECISELY THIS DESIRE POSSIBLE - AND IT WOULD NOT HAVE BEEN NECESSARY TO FULFILL THIS WISH , WE HUMANS HAVE ALREADY BEGUN ABOUT THIS THINKING WAS STOPPED WITH THE PERSON OF JESUS CHRIST , THEN WE HAVE SEIZED THE OPPORTUNITY AND

MADE A GOOD WILL TO
THE DAY - YEAR 1942
TO   REACH   OTHER
PLANETS   TO
COLONIZE THIS , BUT
UNFORTUNATELY   WE
STILL HAVE HUMANS
CONTRIBUTED   TO
MORE HURT BY WAR .

THEREFORE,   THE
TIME   NOW   WAS   NOT
SO LONG AGO , THE
ROOT OF THE CAUSE
TO   BE   REMOVED
FROM   THE   GENE
HISTORY   -   SO   NOW
ALL PEOPLE HAVE TO
HAVE   THE   ABILITY

NOT ONLY TO DIE
AGAIN ALONE WITH
HER WILL OR TO AGE.
BELIEVE IN IT VERY
MUCH DIFFICULT
BECAUSE DIFFERENT
ORGANIZATIONS
REPEATEDLY MADE
FALSE ARBITRARY
TIMES , BECAUSE THE
PEOPLE DID NOT
BELIEVE ...

BUT NOW WAS
CLEARLY EXPLAINED
TO ALL BEINGS IN THE
GLOBAL UNCONSCIOUS

THAT THIS GENETIC MATERIAL FROM THE " FILM OF CREATION" WE IT IS ALSO WRITTEN (BIBLE) , FINALLY REMOVED AND RESHAPED THE WHOLE ESSENCE NOW AS A MAN LIVES .

THEREFORE HAPPEN ON EARTH SINCE 1986 KONERDTOFAGILE DATARSTICHE ELEMENTS THE WAY TO GET EVERYTHING

THERE IS AND
THEREFORE WE HAVE
TO ALL BE THE
CHOICE FOR ALL TIME
- UNFORTUNATELY
THE PLANET ITSELF
HAD REPEATEDLY
KERATINS REASON TO
RESORT TO DRASTIC
MEANS TO AT LEAST
7 BILLION TO GET
PEOPLE / ANIMALS
NOT INCLUDED. FEW
SELECTED PEOPLE
WERE TASKS
HAPPENED TO PASS
THE ESSENCE OF THE
SOCIAL MASS -

DECREASES WITH THE
PURPOSE OF NO
EARTHLY MAN IN
NUMBER. ANYONE CAN
NOW GET FOR ALL
TIME IN AN ETERNAL
BE - TO ACCEPT,
FACILITATED THIS
UNFORTUNATELY "
INCREDIBLE " ARE
CALLED ANDROIDS
BUILT WITH HIGH
PRESSURE - WHICH
ALL PEOPLE WORK
PARTLY STILL
UNFORTUNATELY
NEED TO DO TO
RELEASE - SO THE

THE LIGHTER MAN IN
A UNIT CAN FIND
ENOUGH TIME AND
WILL ONLY HAVE TIME
TO LEARN
THEMSELVES . IN
EVERYTHING WE DO
WE ARE BEING
WATCHED AND WILL
BE DRIVEN BY US
AVERTED .

UNFORTUNATELY, THIS
ALSO LEADS TO
MISUNDERSTANDINGS ,
AS MANY PEOPLE
PERCEIVE WHAT DOES

NOT LEAD TO A SIMPLE DISTRUST .

SUCH SMALL REPORTS ON THE HISTORY OF TIME ARE NECESSARY TO MAKE TODAY SPEAK CONSPICUOUS ENOUGH TO DEEDS THAT WE ALL DO IT YOURSELF . WORK ON GLOBALIZATION IS AND NEVER WAS MUCH NEEDED AS NOW . IF WE DO NOT RECOGNIZE THE NEED FOR

PEOPLE WITH KNOWLEDGE OF THE PLANET WILL TAKE A SELF-SERVING MEASURE FOR YOURSELF AND GET RID OF US .

THEREFORE, WE SHOULD DEFINITELY HELP EACH OTHER AND NOT DISREGARD THE PURE SIMPLE LAWS OF NATURE , NOR DO WE HAVE TO EAT ALL AND DRINK - ALL WE HAVE TO LEARN IS THAT WE ARE ONE WITH EACH

OTHER AND LIVE IN ONE ANOTHER AND WE DO HAVE LONG WITHOUT REALIZING IT .

EACH OF US SHOULD LEARN TO BE CLEAR ABOUT IT, THAT THE DIE HAS AN END AND THIS IS THE REASON TO DEAL WITH EACH OTHER IN FRIENDSHIP .

HELP EACH OTHER AND DO NOT LOOK BACK AND DO THEM AWAY BUT THEY WHAT MUST BE DONE , AND ABOVE ALL HELP

YOU WHERE THEY CAN.

THANK YOU FOR YOUR ATTENTION AND WISH THEM ALWAYS A HAPPY TIME BECAUSE ONLY THE MIND IS WHY THE ONLY PEOPLE LIVING ON THIS PLANET .

THANK YOU

2. LETTER TO MR. W.

LETTER TO A FORMER MANAGER WHO WAS APPOINTED FOR ME BY THE DISTRICT COURT TRUE, HE NEVER WANTED TO BE A MIXED IN MY LIFE, MORE THAN FIVE YEARS HE WAS A FAITHFUL HELPER OF

JUST MY BEST. TODAY, WE STILL KEEP IN TOUCH WITH EACH OTHER AND I HAVE IT MORE THAN YOU! (HE WAS EVEN MY BEST MAN)

DIRK L. FEILER, KAISERSLAUTERN THE 08.01.2005

... HELLO MR. W.

THE   FOLLOWING
STORY IS PURE TRUTH,
IT HAPPENED ...

IT WAS SOMETIME IN
THE 90S, 1995 I THINK
WE   DID   NOT   KNOW,
THE   POLICE   PICKED
ME   UP   IN   THE
MORNING   AND   TOOK

ME TO THE HOSPITAL,
WHERE I CALLED TO
THE HEARING ABOUT
20 LAWYERS, UNTIL
THEN A PROMISED
AND HAS COME .

AROUND 13:00 CLOCK
EVERYTHING WAS
CLARIFIED AND I
WOULD ACTUALLY BE
ALLOWED TO GO
BACK, THEN THE
HEAD DOCTOR PULLED
A MANUSCRIPT FROM
ME FROM THE INSIDE
POCKET OF HIS

JACKET AND ASKED ME IF HE COULD SHOW THIS MANUSCRIPT TO THE JUDGE, I SAID YES, I HAVE NOTHING TO HIDE , THE YOUNG JUDGE FLIPPED AROUND IN IT, IN THIS SCRIPT, AMONG OTHERS, A DREAM TOLD IN WHICH CONCERNED ALIENS HAD THE WEAPONS, SHE ASKED ME: DID THE ALIENS IN YOUR DREAM WEAPONS, I SAID YES. THEN HAD

MY LAWYER AND I LEFT THE ROOM.

WHEN WE WERE CREATED PURELY THE JUDGE HAD DECIDED TO IMPRISON ME FOR SIX WEEKS, ULTIMATELY BECAUSE OF A DREAM IN WHICH ALIENS WEAPONS CARRIED WITH THEM. (A DREAM ABOUT I CARED AND WAS SURPRISED!)

I WAS TAKEN AWAY BY TWO NURSES AND BROUGHT INTO A ROOM

WHERE I WAS TIED TO
THE ARMS AND LEGS
TO A BED, THEN WAS
OFF MY ARM HAIRS
FROM SHAVING, ON
THE SITE OF AN
INFUSION NEEDLE WAS
INSERTED, THEN THE
BOTTLE WAS
ATTACHED AND I
ASKED WITH TEARS IN
MY VOICE THE
DOCTOR, PLEASE
HOLD MY HAND UNTIL I
FELL ASLEEP, I
PASSED OUT, THEY
FILLED ME THIS WISH,
THEN I WAS GONE A

WEEK AND HAVE ONLY FRAGMENTARY MEMORIES. AFTER A WEEK, THE SHACKLES WERE REMOVED AND I WAS ABLE TO MOVE AROUND FREELY AGAIN AND IT WAS OBSERVED A YOUNG APPRENTICE, A NURSE, TOOK ME FOREVER WITH THE NURSES' HOME AND INVITED ME TO SMOKE, (HASH-SMOKING) THAT OFTEN I WAS LATE BACK FROM THE OUTPUT,

THEN I SHOULD DO A DRUG TEST, HIT THE STATION DOCTOR BEFORE WHEN THE HEAD DOCTOR HEARD THAT I OFTEN IN THE HOUSE OF THE PERSONAL WAS THE DRUG TEST HE WAS FORBIDDEN.

THE NEXT DAY I CAME BACK TOTALLY STONED TOO LATE FROM THE OUTPUT BACK AND HAD EVEN MISSED DINNER, I WENT TO THE NURSES' STATION WHERE

25

PRECISELY WAS THE HANDING OVER, EXCEPT STONED I WAS STILL DRUNK, THE YOUNG APPRENTICES DRANK CHAMPAGNE WITH ME FOR SMOKING POT. THE NURSE ASKED ME WHERE I WAS AND I SAID WHEN PATRIK IN THE DORM, EVERYONE LAUGHED LOUDLY AND THEN ASKED IF I STILL WANT TO EAT SOMETHING, I SAID YES, I WANT, I HAVE EATING A FEW

LOAVES AND SEVERAL PUDDINGS, THE NEXT DAY WERE 350 PATIENTS ILL WITH SALMONELLA POISONING. I WAS CONTAMINATED SALMONELLA ALSO THE PUDDING. THE FOLLOWING WEEK WE WERE DOING PATIENTS ALL VERY POOR, I HAD MADE HAD ABOUT 40 FEVER, COLD COMPRESSES, THAT ALWAYS TOOK MY SPECIAL FRIEND WITH WHOM I HAD BEEN

INVITED REGULARLY TO SMOKE, MY DECISION WAS CANCELED, BUT I HAD TO STAY AS LONG UNTIL I WAS NEGATIVE FOR SALMONELLA, WHEN I WAS RELEASED I STILL WEIGHED 65 KG AND WAS A SUPPORT ATTACHED, THE DEAR LORD ESSMÜLLER, THE LITTLE FUCKER, <(COMES FROM SEXUAL MASTURBATION), ("APOLOGY"), (.. .EACH

MAN HAS DONE IT AGAIN, EXCEPT I THINK JESUS AND GOD, THAT MAN CAN NOT STAND THIS IS NOT A MAN IN MY EYES AND THE LITTLE ... JUST A DEFINITION, NOT AN INSULT, SMALL IN TERMS OF POOR / IGNORANT IN SPIRIT, MY SON, I HAD ONE, I'D CALL IT "LITTLE" HE WOULD FEEL "STUPID" ... WHO THEREFORE FEELS HURT IS NOT TO HIS MANHOOD AND IT CAN BE SEEN THAT

THE REAL AND NOT "UPRIGHT" MAN IS THAT HE LACKS SELF-AWARENESS, THAT MY OPINION IS IF SOMEONE FEELS UNDERSTOOD WRONG, ONCE I HAVE A SON TO MY WIFE AND I CALL HIM DREW GORDON ...), IT TOOK THE GREATEST CARE, I HAVE TOLD HIM AGAIN AND AGAIN THAT HE IS A SMALL "WANKER" AND THAT HE WOULD SEE WHAT HE WOULD NEVER

FORGET, HE SHOULD DO SOMETHING AGAINST MY WILL, THEN HE GAVE ME TO YOU AND I WAS SYSTEMATICALLY AUTHORITY OF DRUGS CONDITIONAL ON PREVIOUSLY I REFUSED ANY KIND OF MEDICATION, I AGAIN AND AGAIN SAID, I DO NOT NEED MEDICATION AND I WOULD HAVE NO HAND THAT I HAD EVEN PROVED I WAS A YEAR VOLUNTARILY IN

MERZIG, (PSYCHIATRY),
AND HAVE NOT TAKEN
ANY DRUGS, I RESTED
THERE ONLY FROM
TRYING THE UNUSUAL
IN MY LIFE TO
UNDERSTAND, THEN I
WANTED TO LIVE A
NORMAL LIFE AND
START FROM
SCRATCH AND THAT
UNAIDED, I'M
CERTAINLY NO
WEAKLING OR EVEN
STUPID , CERTAINLY
NOT, I WOULD HAVE
DONE IT TOO WITHOUT
DRUGS, AND WOULD

BE ON, I'M STILL ADDICTED TO DRUGS AND MY ORGANS SUFFER PSYCHOPATHS WHO CALL THEMSELVES DOCTORS DONE BECAUSE I HAD A DREAM CARRIED ME INTO THE ALIEN WEAPONRY.

FOR THIS PAIN I SUFFERED I ASK TODAY THAT THE COMPANY SAFETY ME TO PAY FOR LIFE MONEY FOR MY LIVING, SHOULD I NEED, AND I

WILL NOT LIFT A FINGER WHEN I DO NOT WANT ANYTHING TO WORK FOR THIS MONEY, NOTHING THERE'S, THERE WILL BE DANCING TO MY TUNE, I HAVE BEEN POISONED SO FAR 19 YEARS OF MY LIFE, FOR THIS COMPANY I DO NOTHING, NOTHING AT ALL, I ONLY WORK FOR PEOPLE WHOM I LOVE AND FOR ME!

MORE YOU CAN NOT EXPECT MORE FROM ME!

In the meantime, I made sure that my disability card for the rest of my life is valid! And can I just like the popular Curling reversed !!! (I'm officially retired and got recognized a degree of disability of 70%, ask / judge yourself times even those who caused the mental disorder !?)

AND I MANAGE MY DISCRETION, I HAVE NEVER BEEN "SICK", I WAS TRANSFERRED TO FEAR, ALL I HAD WAS FEAR! FEAR THE STUPIDITY OF THE "PEOPLE".

TODAY, THERE ARE FOR ME THE KIDS I'VE ACTUALLY ALWAYS LOVING, DEEP INSIDE ME, BECAUSE THEY NOTHING FOR THEIR "STUPIDITY / IGNORANCE" CAN.

Until then ...

Greeting Dirk L.
Feiler

YEPPA

www.ingramcontent.com/pod-product-compliance
Lightning Source LLC
Chambersburg PA
CBHW050848290526
45792CB00002B/569